The Library of
HOLIDAYS™

W9-AQQ-523

Memorial Day

Amy Margaret

The Rosen Publishing Group's
PowerKids Press™
New York

For Tyler James

Published in 2002 by The Rosen Publishing Group, Inc.
29 East 21st Street, New York, NY 10010

First Edition

Book Design: Michael Caroleo and Michael de Guzman
Project Editors: Jennifer Landau, Jennifer Quasha, Joanne Randolph

Photo Credits: p. 4 © Allan H. Shoemake/FPG International; p. 7 © Oscar White/CORBIS; p. 8 © Tim Wright/CORBIS; p. 11 © Francis G. Mayer/CORBIS; p. 12 © Richard T. Nowitz/CORBIS; p. 12 (inset) © Joseph Sohm; ChromoSohm/CORBIS; p. 15 © Mark Reinstein/FPG International; p. 16 © Reuters/Chris Kleponis/Archive Photos; p. 19 © AFP/CORBIS; p. 20 © Ralph A. Clevenger/CORBIS; p. 22 © Michael Prince/CORBIS.

Margaret, Amy.
Memorial Day / By Amy Margaret. — 1st ed.
        p.cm.— (The library of the holidays)
Includes bibliographical references and index.
  ISBN 0-8239-5784-5 (lib. bdg.)
1. Memorial Day—Juvenile literature. [1. Memorial Day. 2. Holidays.]
I. Title. II. Series: Margaret, Amy. Library of holidays.
  E642.M5 2002
  394.262—dc21   00–012195

Contents

What Is Memorial Day?

Memorial Day is a day when Americans remember the men and women in the United States **military** who died for their country. This holiday is observed in almost every state on the last Monday in May. People also recognize Memorial Day as the beginning of summer. They celebrate with camp-outs, barbecues, and other outdoor activities. Memorial Day is celebrated everyplace in the world where Americans have died fighting wars.

◀ *On Memorial Day, relatives visit the graves of loved ones who died fighting for their country.*

How Memorial Day Began

The first official Memorial Day was held on May 30, 1868. Flowers were put on the graves of **Civil War** soldiers at Arlington National Cemetery that year. By the next year, people all over the country were honoring dead soldiers on that date. More than 100 years later, in 1971, the date was changed to the last Monday in May.

More than twenty-five towns claim that their town started Memorial Day. In 1966, however, President Lyndon Johnson (right) chose Waterloo, New York, as the official location of the first Memorial Day. ▶

6

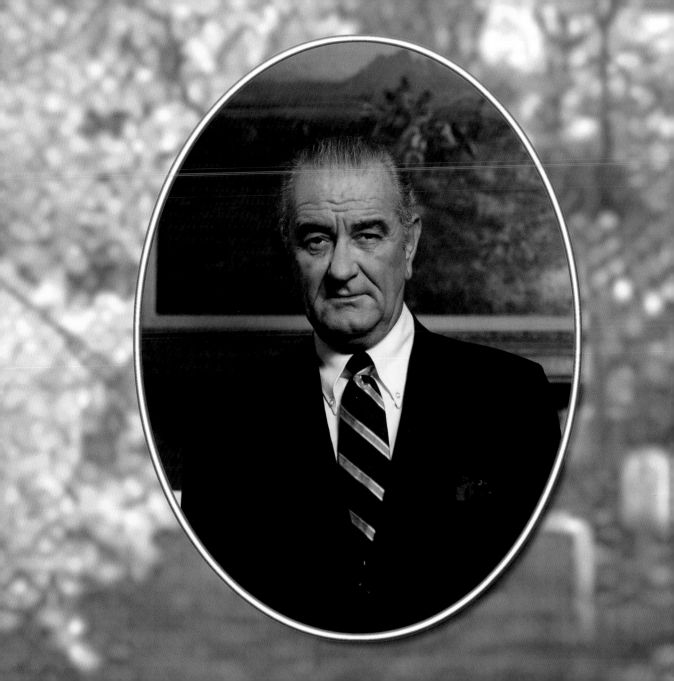

The Confederate Memorial Day

When Memorial Day first began, the southern states didn't take part. They felt that the holiday honored only **Union** soldiers who fought in the Civil War. During the war, the southerners, called **Confederates**, believed that white men had the right to own slaves. In 1918, after World War I, the holiday changed from remembering the Civil War deaths to honoring all Americans who fought in any war. This is when the southern states decided to take part in the holiday.

These men are dressed to look like Confederate soldiers. After the Civil War, the South held its own holiday, called Confederate Memorial Day.

The American Flag

The main symbol for Memorial Day is the American flag. In May 1776, George Washington and two other men asked Betsy Ross to sew a flag for the 13 **colonies** that would become the first American states. There were to be 13 stars to stand for the colonies. The stars were in a circle to show that this new country would be "without end." The flag also had 13 stripes. The white stripes stood for **liberty**.

This is a picture of George Washington, Betsy Ross, and the original 13-star flag. The red stripes on the flag stood for England, the country from which ▶ *most of the settlers had come.*

10

Memorial Day Symbols and Traditions

Another symbol of Memorial Day is the red-paper poppy flower. Red poppies were chosen because they were found growing in the battlefield graveyards in France during World War I. A song that you are likely to hear on Memorial Day is "Taps," which is played on a single bugle. It has been played at all military funerals since 1891. Parades are another popular Memorial Day **tradition**. Many war **veterans** march proudly in their military uniforms.

◀ *This is a picture of a field of red poppies. The small photograph shows a flag and red poppies placed before a memorial to Vietnam War veterans.*

The Arlington National Cemetery has been an official military cemetery since June 15, 1864. Many people who died serving America in a war are buried there. In all, more than 260,000 people are buried at Arlington. Each year, about 5,000 people attend the Memorial Day service, the nation's official way of honoring American service members. Just before the Memorial Day events, American flags are placed by every gravestone. This tradition is called Flags In.

In this picture, a soldier is placing an American flag by a gravestone in a tradition called Flags In. ▶

14

The Tomb of the Unknowns

At the Tomb of the Unknowns in Arlington National Cemetery, three soldiers are buried. They represent every soldier from World War I, World War II, the Korean War, and the Vietnam War whose body could not be identified. In 1998, government officials performed tests that allowed them to identify the Vietnam soldier's remains. He then was reburied near his home. The burial spot for the unknown soldier of the Vietnam War remains empty.

A soldier must pass many tests to be allowed to guard the Tomb of the Unknowns. The Tomb is guarded each day of the year.

17

The National Moment of Remembrance

The National Moment of Remembrance is a time when Americans are asked to take a minute to reflect on the many people who died fighting for our country. During this minute, which takes place at 3:00 P.M. on Memorial Day, people can find the song "Taps" playing on the radio. Others spend this minute in silence. Whatever people do, it is a moment to think about our freedom and those who died to protect us.

This is a picture of a soldier playing "Taps" at Arlington National Cemetery. ▶

18

Remembering Soldiers Around the World

People all over the world have days to remember those who died in battle. Australia honors its veterans on a day called ANZAC Day on April 25. The day marks the time when Australian and New Zealand soldiers first fought in World War I in 1915. Ceremonies are held each year at the Australian War Memorial. During the gathering, the audience observes two minutes of silence for those who died in battle.

◀ *This is a picture of an ANZAC Day parade. ANZAC stands for Australian and New Zealand Army Corps.*

Celebrating Memorial Day Today

There are many ways to celebrate Memorial Day. If your family has an American flag, hang it outside. Visit your local cemetery and place flowers on soldiers' graves. Participate in the National Moment of Remembrance. However you choose to spend your Memorial Day, don't forget to be thankful. We can enjoy the freedom our country has to offer because of the many men and women who died fighting for our country and for us.

Glossary

Civil War (SIH-vul WOR) The war from 1861 to 1865 that was between the Northern states and Southern states in America.

colonies (KAH-luh-neez) Areas in a new country where a large group of people move, who are still ruled by the leaders and laws of their old country.

Confederates (kuhn-FEH-deh-ruts) During the Civil War, the Southerners who wanted their states to be separate from the United States.

liberty (LIH-ber-tee) The power to choose.

military (MIH-lih-ter-ee) Part of the government that protects the United States; the armed forces, such as the army or the navy.

tradition (tra-DIH-shun) A belief or way of doing something that is passed down from family to family.

Union (YOON-yun) During the Civil War, the Northern states that wanted to keep the country together.

veterans (VEH-teh-ruhnz) Men and women who have served in the military.

Index

Web Sites

To learn more about Memorial Day, check out these Web sites:
www.geocities.com/Athens/Acropolis/1465/memorial.html
www.usmemorialday.org